Fiddle Time Run

T0055780

a second book of easy pieces for violin

Kathy and David Blackwell

Illustrations by Martin Remphry

Welcome to **Fiddle Time Runners**. You'll find:

- pieces using the finger patterns 0–12–3–4 and 0–1–2–34
- traditional tunes and pieces by well-known composers from Handel to Mozart
- original pieces in a range of styles from rag to flamenco
- duets, with parts of equal difficulty
- play-along tracks and backing tracks (accompaniment only) available to download from **www.oup.com/ftrunners3e** or to stream on major streaming platforms
- practice tracks recorded at a slower tempo for some pieces
- piano and violin accompaniments available separately
- a book for violin that's also compatible with *Viola Time Runners*; 33 of the 38 tunes may be played together.

OXFORD
UNIVERSITY PRESS

Great Clarendon Street, Oxford OX2 6DP, England
This collection © Oxford University Press 1998, 2003, 2005, 2013, and 2023
Unless marked otherwise, all pieces are by Kathy and David Blackwell and are © Oxford University Press. All traditional pieces, and nos. 12, 14, and 32, are arranged by Kathy and David Blackwell and are © Oxford University Press.
Unauthorized arrangement or photocopying of this copyright material is ILLEGAL.

Kathy and David Blackwell have asserted their right under the Copyright, Designs and Patents Act, 1988, to be identified as the Composers of this Work.

Impression: 1

ISBN: 978-0-19-356609-5

Music and text origination by Julia Bovee
Printed in Great Britain

Contents

Section 1—New notes for second finger **3**

1. Start the show 3
2. Banyan tree (*duet*) 4
3. Heat haze 5
4. Medieval tale 5
5. Cornish May song 6
6. Chase in the dark 6
7. Merrily danced the Quaker's wife 7
8. O leave your sheep (*duet*) 8
9. Jazzy Jingle bells (J. Pierpont) 9
10. Allegretto in G (Mozart) 10
11. The Mallow fling 10
12. Noël (Daquin) (*duet*) 11
13. Finale from the 'Water Music' (Handel) 12
14. Ecossaise in G (Beethoven) 13
15. Fiddle Time rag 14
16. Busy day (*duet*) 15
17. On the go! 16
18. Yodelling song 16
19. Takin' it easy 17
20. Romani band 17
21. Ten thousand miles away (*duet*) 18
22. I got those fiddle blues 20
23. Air in G (J. C. Bach) 21
24. Prelude from 'Te Deum' (Charpentier) 21
25. That's how it goes! 22

Section 2—New notes for third finger **23**

26. Hari coo coo 23
27. Summer evening 23
28. Flamenco dance 24
29. Adam in the garden 25
30. Somebody's knocking at your door 26
31. The old chariot 26
32. Air (Handel) (*duet*) 27
33. The wee cooper o' Fife 28
34. Winter song 28
35. Rory O'More (*duet*) 29
36. Trick cyclist 30
37. Aerobics! 30
38. Caribbean sunshine 31

Music Fact-Finder Page **32**

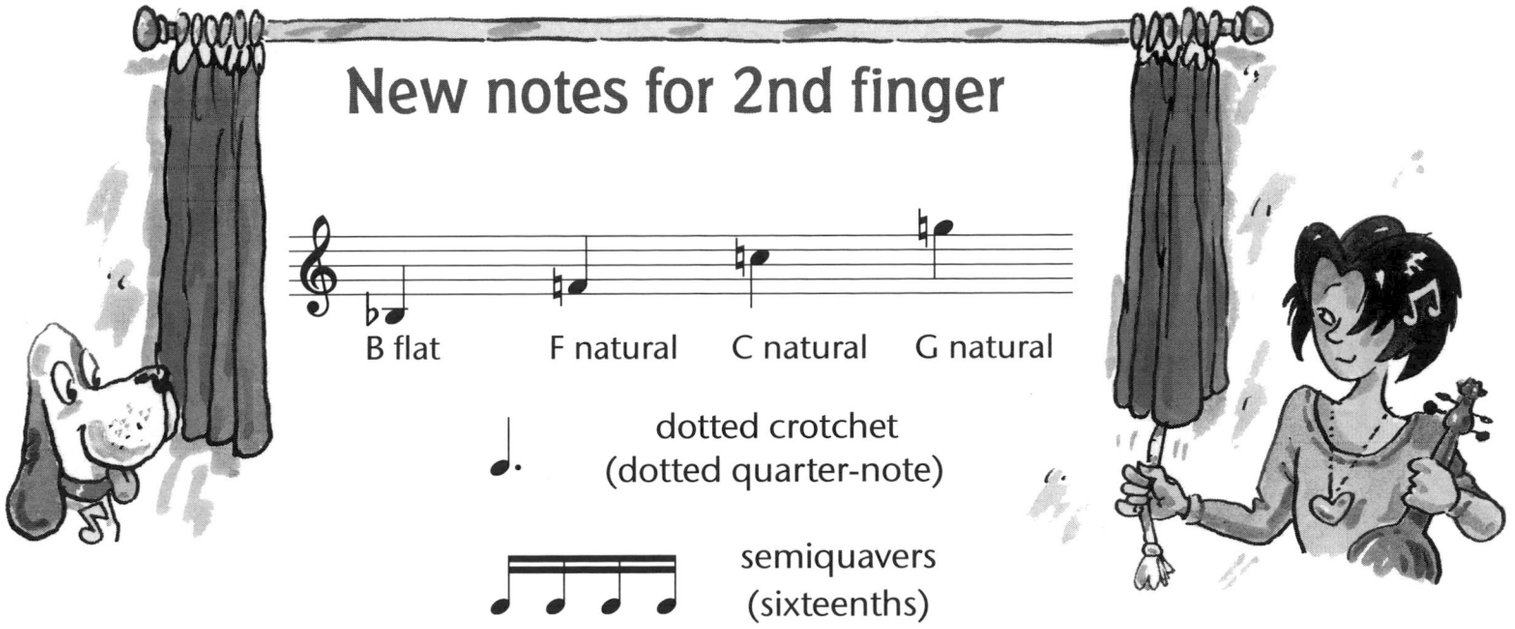

1 Start the show

Count 4 bars

Rock tempo

KB & DB

f

9 *mf*

13 *f*

17 *mf cresc.* *f*

21 *mf*

25 *f*

2 Banyan tree

3 Heat haze

KB & DB

Relaxed

mp

5 *cresc.* *mf*

9 *mp* *mf*

13 pizz.

To practise the main rhythm of this piece, try saying ♩. ♪ ♩ ♩
'Hot and sun - ny.'

4 Medieval tale

KB & DB

Sadly

mp legato

5 *mf* *mp*

9 *mf*

11 **rit.** *mp*

5 Cornish May song

Lively

Cornish folk tune

f

5 *mf*

9 *f*

13 *mf cresc.* *ff*

39 Practice tempo

6 Chase in the dark

Count 2 bars

With menace

KB & DB

f

7 *mp*

11 *mf*

15

19 *f*

23

7 Merrily danced the Quaker's wife

Jig

Scottish folk tune

8 O leave your sheep

French folk tune

9 Jazzy Jingle bells

Count 8 bars

J. Pierpont

Christmassy

10 Allegretto in G

Allegretto

Mozart

mf

f

11 The Mallow fling

Count 2 bars

Lively

Irish folk tune

mf

f

40 Practice tempo

12 Noël
Daquin
Allegretto
f
mf
5
(8)
f
mf
12
f
p
f
15

13 Finale from the 'Water Music'

Handel

14 Ecossaise in G

Beethoven

Allegro

f *mf* 4

7 *f*

12 *mf* 4 4 *f*

17 *mp* *cresc.*

22 *mf* *mp*

27 *cresc.* *f*

15 Fiddle Time rag

Count 4 bars

KB & DB

Not too fast

f

9

13

mf

cresc.

17

f

21

mp

25

29

mf

33

cresc.

f

16 Busy day

Busily
KB & DB
f
mf
f
mf
5
cresc.
cresc.
9
f
p
mp
f
p
mp
14
mf
f
mf
f
19
pizz.
p
pizz.
p

17 On the go!

Count 4 bars

Lively

KB & DB

mf *cresc.*

10 *f* *mp*

15 *cresc.*

20 *f* *mf* *cresc.*

26 *f* pizz.

18 Yodelling song

With a strong beat

German folk tune

f *mf*

6 *mp*

11 *mf*

18 *cresc.* *f*

19 Takin' it easy

Count 4 bars

KB & DB

Laid-back tempo

mp legato

mf

mf

poco rit. **a tempo**

cresc.

mp

mf

pizz.

p

20 Romani band

KB & DB

Fiery!

mf

1.

2.

cresc.

f

sfz

p

cresc.

mf cresc.

ff

41 Practice tempo

21 Ten thousand miles away

21
f
f
D.C. al Fine
25
HOME
10,000 MILES

22 I got those fiddle blues

KB & DB

Slow blues

mf

5

9

13

f *mf*

17

f *mf*

20

f

24

rall.

mp *f*

23 Air in G

24 Prelude from 'Te Deum'

25 That's how it goes!

With energy

KB & DB

f (*p*)

5

(*cresc.*)

Fine

(*f*)

9

mf

13

17

mp

21

cresc.

D.C. al Fine

f

Luckily, this piece is not as hard as it looks!

42 Practice tempo

New notes for 3rd finger

26 Hari coo coo

Count 2 bars

Gently

Indian lullaby

mp

7 **rit.** (2nd time) **Fine**

11 *mf*

15 **D.𝄋 al Fine** *mp*

27 Summer evening

KB & DB

Flowing

mp

6 *mf*

11 **rit.** *mp*

28 Flamenco dance

29 Adam in the garden

Jamaican folk tune

Relaxed tempo

mf cresc. *f*

5 *f*

9

13 *mf*

17

21 *f*

25

29 *f*

33

37 *mp*

41 *f*

30 Somebody's knocking at your door

Spiritual

Gently

p *mp* *mf* *f* *mp* **rit.** *p*

31 The old chariot

Sea shanty

Strongly

f *mf* *f* **Fine** *mf* **D.C. al Fine** *cresc.*

32 Air
Allegro
Handel
f
p
5
9
mf
13
17
21

33 The wee cooper o' Fife

34 Winter song

35 Rory O'More

Lively

Traditional Irish Jig

36 Trick cyclist

With energy

KB & DB

mp *cresc.* *f*

5 *mp* *cresc.* *f*

9 *f* pizz. *p* arco *f*

14 pizz. *p* arco *mp*

19 *cresc.* *f* *mp*

23 *cresc.* *mf cresc.* *f* LH pizz. + + *p*

43 Practice tempo

37 Aerobics!

Fast!

KB & DB

f

5 1. 2. **Fine**

9 *mf*

13 *cresc.* **D.C. al Fine**

38 Caribbean sunshine

KB & DB

Calypso

mf

5

4

8

11

14

f

17

1.

mf

2.

ff

44 Practice tempo

Music Fact-Finder Page

Here are some of the words and signs you will find in some of your pieces!

How to play it

pizzicato or pizz. = pluck
arco = with the bow
⊓ = down bow
V = up bow
> = accent
𝅗𝅥 = tremolo

Don't get lost!

‖: :‖ = repeat marks

1. 2. = first and second time bars

D.C. al Fine = repeat from the beginning and stop at **Fine**
D.𝄋. al Fine = repeat from the sign 𝄋 and stop at **Fine**
rit. or **rall.** = gradually getting slower
a tempo = back to the first speed
𝄐 = pause

Volume control

p (*piano*) = quiet
mp (*mezzo-piano*) = moderately quiet
mf (*mezzo-forte*) = moderately loud
f (*forte*) = loud
ff (*fortissimo*) = very loud

 or *crescendo* (*cresc.*) = getting gradually louder

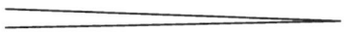 or *diminuendo* (*dim.*) = getting gradually quieter

Italian phrase-book

Allegro = fast and lively
Allegretto = not too fast
Andante = at a walking pace
legato = smoothly
Maestoso = majestically
Moderato = at a moderate speed
Practissimo = lots of Fiddle Time!

Recording credits

Violins: Ros Stephen, Catrin Win Morgan, Marianne Haynes; *Viola*: Felix Tanner; *Cello*: Laura Anstee; *Piano*: David Blackwell, Julian Rowlands; *Drums and percussion*: Andrew Tween; *Accordion*: Pete Rosser; *Guitars*: Kevin Byrne; *Voice*: Lin Marsh, PR, KB
Engineers: Ken Blair, Michael Taylor, Jeff Spencer, Ros Stephen; *Programmer*: Andrew McKenna